W9-CPW-062

RESEARCH TOOL KIT

SMART RESEARCH STRATEGIES

Finding the Right Sources

by Kristine Carlson Asselin

Consultant:
Gwen Hart, PhD
Assistant Professor of English Composition
Buena Vista University
Storm Lake, Iowa

CAPSTONE PRESS
a capstone imprint

Fact Finders are published by Capstone Press,
1710 Roe Crest Drive, North Mankato, Minnesota 56003
www.capstonepub.com

Library of Congress Cataloging-in-Publication Data
Asselin, Kristine Carlson.
  Smart research strategies : finding the right sources / by Kristine Carlson Asselin.
      p. cm.
  Includes bibliographical references and index.
  Summary: "Explores ways to find sources when doing research and writing reports
and other written materials"—Provided by publisher.
  ISBN 978-1-4296-9950-1 (library binding)
  ISBN 978-1-62065-790-4 (paperback)
  ISBN 978-1-4765-1570-0 (ebook PDF)
  1. Report writing—Juvenile literature. 2. Research—Juvenile literature. I. Title.
  LB1047.3.A87 2013
  371.30281—dc23   2012033677

Editorial Credits
Anthony Wacholtz, editor; Juliette Peters, designer; Eric Manske, production specialist

Photo Credits
Alamy: Clark Brennan, 17, Glenn Harper, 16, Lourens Smak, 27, Patrick Eden, 25; Capstone
Press, 15, Capstone Studio/Karon Dubke, 12, 13 (top); Dreamstime: Roland Nagy, 14; Library
of Congress, LC-DIG-ppmsca-19305, 7; Newscom: akg-images, 21; Photodisc, 9; Shutterstock:
Adam Tinney, 18, Amy Johansson, 24, Featureflash, 29, Filip Fuxa, 22, Four Oaks, 4, Henrik
Winther Andersen, 19, Jacek Chabraszewski, 5, Stephaniellen, 23, tuan0989250402, 28,
wavebreakmedia ltd, 13 (bottom)

Artistic Effects
Shutterstock: blue67design, Erica Truex, MisterElements

Printed in the United States of America in North Mankato, Minnesota.
092012   006933CGS13

TABLE OF CONTENTS

Where to Start?

You have a research project for school due in three weeks. It might be a paper about the life of Abraham Lincoln. It could be a poster with information and pictures showing the life cycle of the dung beetle. Maybe it's a diorama of the Grand Canyon or a timeline of the Civil War. Whatever the topic or format, you're going to be elbow deep in research. But where do you start? There are tons of sources out there for you to use—you just need to know where to look!

Research is fun if you know the basics. It's like being the detective of your own mystery. Putting the clues together to create a finished product feels great! But before you dive into solving the mystery and finding your sources, you need some answers.

Starting the Investigation

STEP 1

Know what the teacher wants. Before you begin you need to understand the instructions. When is the project due? How long should it be? Does your teacher have rules on the number or types of sources you need?

STEP 2

Pick your topic. Your teacher might assign a specific topic. If not, you can do some investigating to choose your own subject. Whatever the topic, focus on a specific part that interests you. For example, if your topic is Abraham Lincoln, you could cover his early career as a lawyer, his time in the White House, or his famous speeches. Think about bouncing ideas off a parent, guardian, or classmate.

STEP 3

Make a list. Before you start looking for sources, make a list of research questions. What do you need to know about your topic? This type of early planning is called prewriting and can help you create your outline.

An outline is a short summary of what you plan to write. Some outlines include only the major points of your project. Other outlines are more detailed. As you do more research, you can add paragraphs or bullet points to your outline. You might start by creating an informal outline—a list of basic information organized into **chronological** order. As you dig deeper into your research, you might create a formal outline with more information. Some teachers might require that you submit an outline before you turn in your final paper or project.

PRACTICE EXERCISE

Create an Outline

Read a short biography of a famous American. Make a chronological list of key moments in his or her life. What else do you want to know about the person? Add those questions to your outline.

Abraham Lincoln

chronological—describes a list in which the events are listed in the order they occur

CHAPTER ONE

Where's the Info?

Now that you're clear on the instructions and you've got your outline, it's time to build a **bibliography**. Make a list of possible sources from your preliminary research. Be sure to include books, websites, magazine articles, and anything else that might apply to your topic.

Begin the Search

 STEP 1 Look back at the list of research questions. You'll focus your research on finding the answers.

 STEP 2 Call in backup. Ask a librarian to point out good library sources.

 STEP 3 Consult other books or sources. Most nonfiction books have a bibliography in the back. This list cites the sources an author used in his or her research. You might want to use them in your research too.

bibliography—an alphabetical list of sources used

Librarians to the Rescue!

Librarians are a secret weapon for research!
Your librarian can help identify topics that interest
you or suggest the best sources for you to use.
The librarian can also help you with online tools
available only at the library or through library access.

LIBRARY DATABASE SEARCH

Library databases are a great way to quickly search for books or magazine articles on your topic. Type in some keywords, and the database will give you information about titles that match your search. You'll get the author, title, publisher, and publication date for each of the titles that match. Keep in mind library databases don't work like Internet search engines. You might have to get creative with your keyword choices. For example, instead of just searching for "movie," you might also try "film" and "motion picture."

You might have to connect your keywords if you have more than one. Using "and" between two or more words will narrow the range of titles you'll get. Using "not" with keywords will narrow your search even more. Using "or" between keywords will broaden your search. For example, if you search for bears OR tigers, the results will include books that include either animal. If you search for bears AND tigers, you'll only get books that discuss both animals. If you search for bears NOT tigers, the list will include books on bears, but only if the books don't mention tigers.

Search For

	Subject ⬍	bears
AND ⬍	Subject ⬍	tigers
NOT ⬍	Subject ⬍	cheetahs
AND ⬍	Subject ⬍	

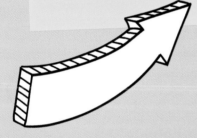

You can also use symbols to expand your search. A common symbol is an asterisk (*). Adding an asterisk to a keyword will bring back results with related words. For example, typing "child*" will include results with child, children, child's, children's, or childhood. Different databases might use other symbols, so check with your librarian.

There are many types of sources. Although you'll probably use websites and books most often, try to use as many kinds of sources as you can. The type of sources you use will also depend on what information you need.

INTERNET SITES

The Internet is loaded with information. In fact, you might use a search engine as the first step in your research. But some of the information on the Internet is misleading or incorrect. Google and other search engines can return millions of websites from just one search. How do you know which websites you can trust? It's usually safe to use information from well-known organizations, such as museums or universities. If you're not sure about a website, check with your teacher. Never give out your name or other personal information online unless your teacher or guardian says it's OK.

BOOKS

Before the Internet, researchers used books as their most common source. Today, you might use more websites in your research. However, your teacher will probably want you to use a few books as well. You can use the library database or browse the shelves to find the ones that work best for you.

Don't worry about reading the whole book! Most of the time, you can find the information you need on just a few pages. Use the index or ask your librarian for help.

PODCASTS AND INTERVIEWS

A podcast is an audio or video recording you can download to a computer or MP3 player. A few years ago, podcasts didn't exist. But now they are a great source for certain types of information. For example, if you're looking for a current interview from an expert on space, NASA has a weekly podcast. There are podcasts on all sorts of topics, from history and art to politics and popular television shows.

NEWSPAPERS—PRINT AND ONLINE

Newspaper articles are usually written at the time an event occurs. They are perfect for current events, such as a presidential election, or a natural disaster, such as a hurricane. When you're researching history, it can also be helpful to use articles from the time period you're studying. A 100-year-old newspaper article will give you a different view than a modern book about the same

event. Pictures of old newspapers and magazines are sometimes stored on rolls of film called microfilm and microfiche. You can find these at your library. The Internet may also have current or past editions available.

ENCYCLOPEDIAS

Encyclopedias are books or series of books that contain brief entries on a wide variety of topics. Encyclopedia Britannica, the oldest English-language encyclopedia, was first published in 1768. You can still find encyclopedias in your library, but they can also be found on the Internet. In fact, in 2012, Encyclopedia Britannica stopped publishing its multivolume sets after 244 years. The company continues to publish its educational information online.

ALMANACS

An almanac is a magazine or newspaper that records information about the sky and the weather. For example, an almanac may report the phases of the moon or the time the sun rises each morning. It may also publish times of the tides, predictions of the weather, and other data related to time. Some almanacs might also have recipes, suggestions for planting and harvesting, and other tips related to agriculture.

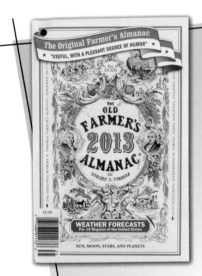

The Old Farmer's Almanac

The Old Farmer's Almanac is North America's oldest continuously published almanac. First created in 1792, it is still published today in Dublin, New Hampshire. The first issue was printed during George Washington's first term as president. The almanac has had only 13 editors since that time. The current editor is Janice Stillman, the almanac's first female editor.

MAGAZINES

Magazines are often called periodicals. They are published on a regular schedule, such as weekly or monthly. Magazines contain articles or essays, usually by more than one author. Most magazines specialize in a particular topic, such as sports, current events, or hobbies. Like newspapers, old editions of magazines can be found on microfiche or microfilm and sometimes online. Newer editions are also often available online.

INTERLIBRARY LOANS

Some libraries participate in interlibrary loan (ILL) programs. These programs allows libraries to share resources. People from one library can check out books from another library. ILL is a great opportunity to use sources your local library might not own. The library will let you know when the book arrives so you can pick it up. You can also request articles through ILL. Many of the articles are electronic, so you can get them in no time! Ask your librarian to show you how to use ILL.

Keep Track!

Keep a record of each source you use—on index cards, in a notebook, or on your computer. One way to stay organized is to print out articles or email them to yourself. That way they'll be handy if you need to use them later.

Wherever you keep your notes, include the following information from each source for your bibliography:

1 The author's name, last name first.

2 The title of the book or article.

3 The title of the periodical, if the source is a newspaper or magazine.

4 The publication information, including the city of publication, publisher, and year of publication.

5 Any notes that may be important to the source.

PRACTICE EXERCISE

Comparing Sources

1. Pick your favorite animal species.
2. Compare three sources on the subject, including at least one book and one website.
   a. How similar is the information included in each source?
   b. Did any of the sources have details that the others didn't?
   c. Did any of the sources have information that disagreed with the others?

CHAPTER TWO

Primary Vs. Secondary Sources

Depending on your project, you are probably going to use a variety of sources. Try not to limit yourself to only books or Internet sources—mix it up! Using a variety of sources is also a good way to **verify** your facts.

PRIMARY SOURCES

A primary source is an eyewitness account of an event. It is usually written or recorded at the time the event occurred. Types of primary sources include diaries, speeches, autobiographies, interviews, and letters. A video recording of Martin Luther King's "I Have a Dream" speech or *The Diary of Anne Frank* are examples of primary sources.

Using primary sources in your research can help you better understand the subject and make your project stronger. Ask your librarian to help you find these sources online or in the library.

verify—to make sure that something is true

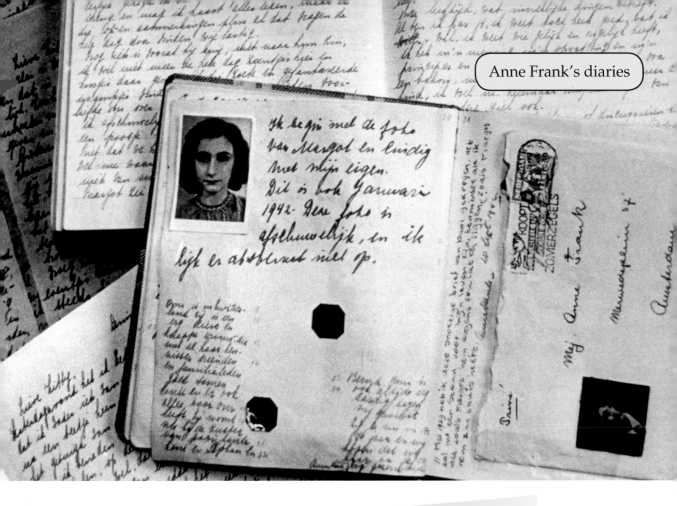

Interviews

Your best primary sources could be right in front of
you. You can interview people who know about the
topic you are researching. For example, your friend's
mother might be an expert gardener. She would be
a great source for information about pesticides or
the right time to plant a vegetable garden. If your
grandfather served in the Vietnam War, he could
tell you what it was like to fight in a war.

SECONDARY SOURCES

Secondary sources are documents based on primary sources. Secondary sources include books, websites, encyclopedias, and dictionaries. An article that discusses the meaning of Martin Luther King's famous speech is an example of a secondary source.

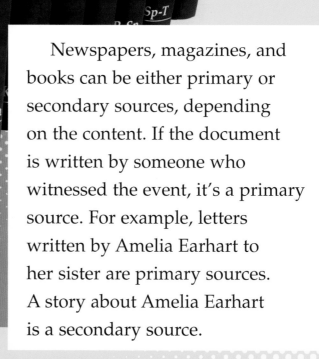

Newspapers, magazines, and books can be either primary or secondary sources, depending on the content. If the document is written by someone who witnessed the event, it's a primary source. For example, letters written by Amelia Earhart to her sister are primary sources. A story about Amelia Earhart is a secondary source.

Identifying Primary and Secondary Sources

Look at the following list of sources. Identify which are primary sources and which are secondary sources.

1. The handwritten diary of a soldier who fought at Gettysburg during the Civil War.

2. An online article retelling personal stories from the battlefield at Gettysburg.

3. A documentary about orangutans, narrated by a scientist who observed the animals in the wild for six months.

4. A televised interview of a person who witnessed a car accident.

5. A biography of Abraham Lincoln written in 2010.

6. Letters about Abraham Lincoln written by his wife during the time of his presidency.

7. A podcast from a volcanologist who witnessed a volcano eruption in August 2012.

Answers: 1) primary, 2) secondary, 3) primary, 4) primary, 5) secondary, 6) primary, 7) primary

CHAPTER THREE

CHAPTER THREE

Evaluating Sources

As you've probably realized, there are millions of sources for researchers to use. Unfortunately, they are not all accurate. You might have to use a bit of investigative skill to figure out which sources are reliable.

First check the date. Is the source current? Then check to see if the author has any **expertise** in the subject. On the Internet, stick with websites by organizations well-known in their field of study. Examples of organizations with **credible** websites include the Wildlife Conservation Society and the National Audubon Society.

expertise—special skill or knowledge
credible—worthy of being believed; trustworthy

Determining Author Credibility

Credible sources can be tricky to identify. Check the following:

1 What type of publication is the source? Books are likely to be more credible than online articles that don't have an author listed.

2 What type of experience does the author have with the subject? Look at the biographical information on the author. If the author's life work is American history, her book on the life of George Washington is probably credible.

3 Who is the publisher? Check to see if the publishing company is known for quality work. If so, the company will make sure the facts are correct before publishing.

Determining Website Credibility

For Internet sources, keep in mind the notes on the previous page as well as these additional concerns:

1 Who's the author? If the author is listed, there will often be contact information.

2 Who hosts the website? The article is likely to be credible if it is hosted by a trustworthy organization. The Smithsonian Institution and the Library of Congress are credible organizations.

3 When was the website created? Has it been recently updated?

You should question the source's credibility if ...

1 No author is listed.

2 There is no bibliography. Without a bibliography, it's more difficult to double-check information.

3 Links on a website are broken or lead to something inappropriate.

4 Advertisements on a website point to the author making money from his or her opinion.

WIKIPEDIA

Wikipedia is an online database that anyone with Internet access can change. Many Wikipedia articles are footnoted. But for most projects, Wikipedia is not an appropriate source. Because anyone can change the information, there's a chance it could be wrong. However, Wikipedia is great as part of a brainstorming strategy or to locate additional sources. Look at the footnotes at the bottom of any Wikipedia entry to see the sources used by the author. If the sources can be found online, you can click on the links to go directly to them.

Plagiarism

When you use someone else's facts or ideas, note the source where you found the information. If you don't give proper credit, you might find yourself being accused of **plagiarism**. Plagiarism in school could get you a failing grade, or in some cases, suspended or expelled. So make sure you give credit where credit is due!

plagiarism—using the thoughts or words of another person and presenting them as your own

27

Finishing the Investigation

So you've got your topic. Your outline and bibliography are written. You've got all the sources you need. Now you can dive into your sources and learn more about your topic! As you read, you can fill in your outline with more details and make changes if necessary. After you've collected all the information you need, you can finally start writing your paper or creating your project. As you write, revise your earlier lists and combine your notes.

With the investigating skills of an expert researcher, you're on your way to a great grade on all your research projects. Your writing will come alive with accurate and detailed information!

PRACTICE EXERCISE

Internet Credibility

Type the name of your favorite celebrity into a search engine. Look at the top five websites. Are they credible? How do you know?

GLOSSARY

bibliography (bib-lee-OG-ruh-fee)—an alphabetical list of sources used

chronological—(kron-uh-LOJ-uh-kuhl) describes a list in which the events are listed in the order they occur

credible (KRED-uh-buhl)—worthy of being believed; trustworthy

expertise (EK-sper-teess)—a special skill or knowledge about a certain subject

footnote (FOOT-noht)—a note at the bottom of a page or document that provides the source or more information about something in the main text

plagiarism (PLAY-juh-riz-uhm)—using the thoughts or words of another person and presenting them as your own

primary source (PRYE-mair-ee SORSS)—source from someone who experienced an event firsthand

secondary source (SEK-uhn-der-ee SORSS)—an interpretation of an event from someone who did not witness it firsthand

verify (VAIR-ih-fye)—to make sure that something is true

READ MORE

Cefrey, Holly. *Researching People, Places, and Events.* Digital and Information Literacy. New York: Rosen Central, 2010.

Gaines, Ann. *Ace Your Research Paper.* Ace It! Berkeley Heights, N.J.: Enslow Publishers, 2009.

Gilbert, Sara. *Write Your Own Article: Newspaper, Magazine, Online.* Write Your Own. Mankato, Minn.: Compass Point Books, 2009.

Hamen, Susan E. *Google: The Company and Its Founders.* Technology Pioneers. Edina, Minn.: ABDO Publishing, 2011.

INTERNET SITES

FactHound offers a safe, fun way to find Internet sites related to this book. All of the sites on FactHound have been researched by our staff.

Here's all you do:

Visit *www.facthound.com*

Type in this code: 9781429699501

Super-cool stuff!

Check out projects, games and lots more at
www.capstonekids.com

INDEX